OECD Regulatory Enforcement and Inspections Toolkit

This work is published under the responsibility of the Secretary-General of the OECD. The opinions expressed and arguments employed herein do not necessarily reflect the official views of OECD member countries.

This document, as well as any data and any map included herein, are without prejudice to the status of or sovereignty over any territory, to the delimitation of international frontiers and boundaries and to the name of any territory, city or area.

Please cite this publication as:
OECD (2018), *OECD Regulatory Enforcement and Inspections Toolkit*, OECD Publishing, Paris.
https://doi.org/10.1787/9789264303959-en

ISBN 978-92-64-30394-2 (print)
ISBN 978-92-64-30395-9 (PDF)

The statistical data for Israel are supplied by and under the responsibility of the relevant Israeli authorities. The use of such data by the OECD is without prejudice to the status of the Golan Heights, East Jerusalem and Israeli settlements in the West Bank under the terms of international law.

Photo credits: Cover © EtiAmmos / Shutterstock.com

Foreword

Regulations are indispensable for the proper function of economies and the society. They create the "rules of the game" for citizens, business, government and civil society. They underpin markets, protect the rights and safety of citizens and ensure the delivery of public goods and services. The objective of regulatory policy is to ensure that regulations and regulatory frameworks work effectively in the public interest.

The way in which regulations are designed is a major factor in both the quality of the regulatory environment for businesses and citizens and the outcomes achieved. But how regulations are implemented and enforced, and how compliance with regulatory requirements is assured and promoted, are also critical determinants of whether the regulatory system is working as intended.

Inspections are one of the most important ways to enforce regulations and to ensure regulatory compliance. As already shown by the *OECD Best Practice Principles for Regulatory Enforcement and Inspections* (OECD, 2014[1]), there are many core activities that inspections have in common and that are relevant for all or most sectors where inspections take place. These issues include planning and better targeting inspections, communicating with regulated subjects, preventing corruption, and promoting ethical behaviour, as well as the organisation of inspections and the governance of inspection authorities.

The *OECD Regulatory Enforcement and Inspections Toolkit* presents a checklist of 12 criteria to help officials, regulators, stakeholders and experts assess the level of development of the inspection and enforcement system in a given jurisdiction, or of a particular institution or structure, to identify strengths and weaknesses, and potential areas for improvement.

The Toolkit builds on previous work by the OECD to promote regulatory reform and the implementation of sound regulatory practices across the whole of government. The body of information and experience it has gathered is summarised in the *Recommendation of the Council on Regulatory and Policy Governance* (OECD, 2012[2]).

Acknowledgements

These principles have been prepared by Daniel Trnka, OECD Senior Policy Analyst, in co-operation with Florentin Blanc, consultant and specialist on business inspection reforms, under the supervision of Nick Malyshev, Head of the Regulatory Policy Division, and Marcos Bonturi, Director of the OECD Public Governance Directorate. Jennifer Stein co-ordinated the editorial process. Thanks are extended to all members of the Regulatory Policy Committee and the Network of Economic Regulators who provided substantial comments and support to the various drafts of the Toolkit.

Extensive and useful comments were also received through public consultations, including from the Ministry of Finance and Public Function, Spain; the Dutch Ministry of Economic Affairs and Climate; the Government of Japan; the French Energy Regulatory Authority; the Brazilian National Metrology, Quality and Technology Institute; Paul van Dijk, Mindert Mulder and Rob Velders, the Netherlands; and Aute Kasdorp, Supervision Strategy, the Netherlands.

Table of contents

Executive summary

The OECD Regulatory Enforcement and Inspections Toolkit is based on the 2014 *OECD Best Practice Principles for Regulatory Enforcement and Inspections* (OECD, 2014[1]). It offers government officials, regulators, stakeholders and experts – including the OECD Secretariat itself – a simple tool for assessing the level of development of the inspection and enforcement system in a given jurisdiction, institution or structure, to identify strengths and weaknesses as well as areas for improvement.

The document presents a checklist of 12 criteria that correspond to the 11 OECD *Best Practice Principles for Regulatory Enforcement and Inspections* (OECD, 2014[1]) plus a twelfth criterion for a "reality check" of actual performance. These criteria are divided into sub-criteria to make them easier to use.

The 12 criteria are:

1. **Evidence-based enforcement:** Regulatory enforcement and inspections should be evidence-based and measurement-based: deciding what to inspect and how should be grounded in data and evidence, and results should be evaluated regularly.

2. **Selectivity:** Promoting compliance and enforcing rules should be left to market forces, private sector actions and civil society activities wherever possible: inspections and enforcement cannot take place everywhere and address everything, and there are many other ways to achieve regulations' objectives.

3. **Risk focus and proportionality**: Enforcement needs to be risk-based and proportionate: the frequency of inspections and the resources employed should be proportional to the level of risk, and enforcement actions should aim at reducing the actual risk posed by infractions.

4. **Responsive regulation**: Enforcement should be based on "responsive regulation" principles; that is, inspection enforcement actions should be modulated depending on the profile and behaviour of specific businesses.

5. **Long-term vision**: Governments should adopt policies on regulatory enforcement and inspections, and establish institutional mechanisms with clear objectives and a long-term strategy.

6. **Co-ordination and consolidation**: Inspection functions should be co-ordinated and, where needed, consolidated: less duplication and fewer overlaps will ensure a better use of public resources, minimise the burden on regulated subjects, and maximise effectiveness.

7. **Transparent governance**: Governance structures and human resources policies for regulatory enforcement should support transparency, professionalism, and results-oriented management. The execution of regulatory enforcement should be independent from political influence, and compliance promotion efforts should be rewarded.

8. **Information integration**: Information and communication technologies should be used to maximise a focus on risks, promote co-ordination and information-sharing and ensure an optimal use of resources.

9. **Clear and fair process**: Governments should ensure that rules and processes for enforcement and inspections are clear. Coherent legislation to organise inspections and enforcement needs to be adopted and published, and the rights and obligations of officials and of businesses, clearly articulated.

10. **Compliance promotion**: Transparency and compliance should be promoted through the use of appropriate instruments such as guidance, toolkits and checklists.

11. **Professionalism**: Inspectors should be trained and managed to ensure professionalism, integrity, consistency and transparency. This requires substantial training focusing not only on technical but also on generic inspection skills, and official guidelines for inspectors to help ensure consistency and fairness.

12. **Reality check**: Institutions in charge of inspection and enforcement, and the regulatory enforcement and inspection system as a whole, should deliver the levels of performance expected from them – in terms of stakeholder satisfaction, efficiency (benefits/costs), and overall effectiveness (safety, health, environmental protection etc.).

The Toolkit is designed to evaluate the *de facto* situation of a given country or institution. To this end, and to make the most effective use of the Toolkit, reviewed countries and institutions should provide concrete evidence for meeting each of the sub-criteria, such as official documents, description of institutional mechanisms in place or concrete data on inspections and their results.

Introduction

The *OECD Regulatory Enforcement and Inspections Toolkit* is based on the *OECD Best Practice Principles for Regulatory Enforcement and Inspections* (OECD, 2014[1]). The purpose of the Toolkit is to build on the Principles to offer government officials, regulators, stakeholders and experts as well as the OECD Secretariat itself a simple tool that allows assessing the level of development of the inspection and enforcement system in a given jurisdiction, or of a particular institution or structure, to identify strengths and weaknesses, and potential areas for improvement.

The Toolkit is not be in any way binding for OECD countries. We acknowledge that there are significant differences between jurisdictions in how regulatory enforcement is organised. In many jurisdictions, there are shared competences in enforcing regulations between the centre and the sub-national levels of the government, sometimes semi- or fully autonomous from the central level. When evaluating enforcement and inspection systems using the Toolkit, such differences and specifics must be taken into account. The Toolkit should, however, form a universal and sufficiently flexible basis for evaluation and self-assessment.[1] We hope that during the process of testing the Toolkit in practice, it will be enriched by examples of good practices in meeting selected sub-criteria.

The document presents a "checklist" composed of 12 criteria that correspond to the 11 *OECD Best Practice Principles for Regulatory Enforcement and Inspections*, and a twelfth criterion for a "reality check" of actual performance. These criteria are themselves divided into sub-criteria to make them easier to use.

Assessing inspection and enforcement institutions and systems is complex: it involves looking at legislation, institutional structures, staff and practices, across a number of regulatory areas, sectors etc. Many criteria are not easily translated into directly measurable indicators, and even when they can be, data is not always readily available. The use of such a "check-list" and of its different indicators thus involves a significant degree of expert judgment, and is more "qualitative" than "quantitative". To make it easier to use and more reliable, the sub-criteria are as precisely defined as possible, and are clarified through guidance on how to understand and assess them.

A good inspection and enforcement system should simultaneously aim at delivering the best possible outcomes in terms of risk prevention or mitigation and promoting economic prosperity, enhancing welfare and pursuing the public interest (OECD, 2012[2]) (such as, for example, improving the quality of the environment, public safety and health, quality of education, etc.), doing so without exceedingly increasing costs for the state and burden for regulated subjects, and ensure trust and satisfaction from different stakeholders, whose perspectives are often conflicting (businesses, civil society organisations etc.).

---

1.   Where relevant international agreements/standards/recommendations exist for governments to use with respect to the inspection and enforcement system of each specific sector, they take precedence over this toolkit.

This is not only challenging to achieve, but also difficult to measure. First, because data is often unavailable, or not necessarily reliable, due to limitations in measurement methods. Second, because even if data is available and trusted, inspections and enforcement only have very indirect effects on the indicators that would be most relevant to the regulatory goals.

For instance, food safety regulations aim at reducing deaths and diseases due to food-borne illnesses – but regulations, inspections and enforcement are only one of the many factors affecting whether food is safe. Inspectors neither prepare, nor consume the food – safety is in the hands of all stakeholders, including producers, distributors and consumers. Inspections and enforcement can only attempt to influence behaviours that themselves will contribute to the desired goals. Thus, changes in key public welfare indicators are difficult to attribute directly to changes in inspections and enforcement.

For all these reasons, it is important to use the different criteria and sub-criteria together, and not in isolation. Good results in one area may not be fully meaningful if performance in other areas is poor. High efficiency may not be a good thing if it means reduced effectiveness – and high effectiveness without regard to the costs will be unsustainable.

In considering whether a system or an institution fulfils a given sub-criterion, users of this check-list should consider a gradation of ratings rather than a binary answer. If the sub-criterion is met only very rarely, or to a very small extent, or by a small minority of inspection and enforcement structures, the rating is overall negative. If the sub-criterion is fulfilled by a fair share of institutions but far from all, or important parts of it are met but significant shortcomings still exist, the rating can be considered as "intermediate". If it is met by the overwhelming majority of institutions or in most cases, or most of its points are met (even if some areas exist for improvement), the rating will be positive. We do not offer here a specific rating system, but depending on the level of detail sought there could be at least 3 ratings (poor, average, good) or (offering more nuance) 5 ratings (from very poor to very good).

Definition of some key terms

In accordance with the *OECD Best Practice Principles for Regulatory Enforcement and Inspections*, "enforcement" will be taken in its broad meaning, covering all activities of state structures (or structures delegated by the state) aimed at promoting compliance and reaching regulations' outcomes – e.g. lowering risks to safety, health and the environment, ensuring the achievement of some public goods including state revenue collection, safeguarding certain legally recognised rights, ensuring transparent functioning of markets etc. These activities may include: information, guidance and prevention; data collection and analysis; inspections; enforcement actions in the narrower sense, i.e. warnings, improvement notices, fines, prosecutions etc. To distinguish the two meanings of enforcement, "regulatory enforcement" will refer to the broad understanding, and "enforcement actions" to the narrower sense.

"Inspections" will be understood as any type of visit or check conducted by authorised officials on products or business premises, activities, documents etc.

"Risk" should be understood here as the combination of the likelihood of an adverse event (hazard, harm) occurring, and of the potential magnitude of the damage caused (itself combining the number of people affected, and severity of the damage for each).

Source: (OECD, 2014[1]), *Regulatory Enforcement and Inspections*, OECD Best Practice Principles for Regulatory Policy, OECD Publishing, Paris, http://dx.doi.org/10.1787/9789264208117-en.

Criterion 1. Evidence-based enforcement[1]

Regulatory enforcement and inspections should be evidence-based and measurement-based: deciding what to inspect and how should be grounded on data and evidence, and results should be evaluated regularly.

Key questions:

- Are enforcement and inspection aspects reviewed during Impact Assessment for regulations, and considered in *ex post* review of regulations?

- Do the mandates of regulatory enforcement and inspections institutions reflect goals set by governments in terms of risk reduction and pursuing public interest?

- Do the indicators and data used to assess the performance of regulatory enforcement and inspections institutions similarly focus on outcomes such as risk reduction, economic growth, social well-being etc.?

- Are effectiveness evaluations implemented in practice, and do they have real consequences in terms of inspection and enforcement structures, methods, resources and tools?

---

1.   i.e. grounded in the best available research and existing data and informed by Impact Assessment, cost-benefit analysis, experiential evidence from the field and relevant contextual evidence.

Sub-criterion 1.1. Enforcement and inspection aspects are reviewed during the Impact Assessment process for new regulations – and evidence-based enforcement is "anchored" as a key aspect to be checked during both design and ex post *review of regulations*

Considering the implementation and enforcement stage of proposed regulations is an integral part of "best practice" Regulatory Impact Assessment (and Impact Assessment more broadly). In principle, *ex post* reviews should also be looking at enforcement and broader implementation questions. However, available evidence suggests that specific attention is not always paid to these issues. Many RIAs treat inspections and enforcement as a given, something that more-or-less automatically should or will happen (and be effective), rather than specifically considering the different possible options, their costs and benefits, as well as their relative effectiveness (or lack thereof). Likewise, *ex post* reviews often look at the cost and effectiveness of a given regulation *as a whole*, without considering the inspection and enforcement part in its specificity, looking at whether it was correctly designed and implemented, what would be the alternatives etc. Feedback is also not always sought from the inspectors themselves, or from stakeholders specifically on the topic of inspections and enforcement.

In order for the inspection and enforcement system to be adequately designed and achieve the best balance of efficiency and effectiveness, it is necessary to properly consider whether inspections and enforcement would be needed for a proposed regulation, how they should be organised and resourced, what methods they should follow.[2] These same issues should be considered when reviewing regulations *ex post*.

- *Evidence: RIA guidelines/procedures, contents of published RIAs*

Sub-criterion 1.2. The mandates of institutions in charge of regulatory enforcement and inspections reflect goals in terms of risk reduction and pursuing public interest

There should be no automatic assumption that enforcing a given set of legislation requires an ad hoc institution – and that "enforcing legislation" is an adequate definition of purpose. Rather, institutions empowered to inspect and enforce should have a purpose that is stated in terms of what harm to the public they will mitigate, of what positive outcomes they will contribute to achieve. Institutions, that are not able to define their mission in this way, typically create significant costs without clear benefits, and have little incentives to improve approaches and methods to achieve better results. Nor is it possible to properly assess their performance, since it is defined in a purely "circular" way: their task is to inspect and enforce, the more they do of it, the better, regardless of what benefits or costs this entails for the public.

---

2.   See e.g. the Netherlands' "Table of Eleven" (as in www.oecd.org/gov/regulatory-policy/44912386.pdf), in (OECD, 2010[3]).

It is thus essential that each institution or structure with inspection and enforcement power have a mandate that is clearly defined in terms of risk management[3] and/or outcomes for social well-being to which it should contribute. The mandates can be set in a variety of ways (generally through primary or secondary legislation, but they can also be supplemented through strategy documents approved by the supervisory board or ministry etc.).

- *Evidence: official mandates as adopted in relevant legislation/official documents*

Sub-criterion 1.3. Do the indicators and data used to assess the performance of regulatory enforcement and inspections institutions similarly focus on outcomes such as risk reduction, economic growth, social well-being etc.?

Using volume of activities (inspections) or violations detected (and sanctions) as indicators gives perverse incentives to inspecting agencies, since they then have an incentive to achieve low compliance levels, which will give them more volume – and runs contrary to their mission. Performance should be assessed against the achievement of social well-being (safety, health, environmental protection etc.) and, as an intermediate step towards this and a proxy for these goals, against improvements in compliance. It is indispensable that this be defined as a central task and indicator for inspection and enforcement structures.

Just as mandates set for enforcement and inspections institutions need to correspond to improvements in social well-being and reductions in risk levels, specific objectives and indicators defined to measure performance within these mandates should have a similar focus. For each specific inspectorate and enforcement area, key indicators can be identified that relate meaningfully to their mandate. This can be done by first defining a number of high-level "goals", "aims" or "priority areas" (since most inspectorates are responsible for a broad regulatory domain that covers several distinct goals) and, within each of these, specific objectives and indicators measuring to what extent these objectives are being achieved. Because there are a number of issues involved in properly measuring outcomes from inspections and enforcement activities (attribution problems, problematic quality of data in some cases, difficulty to measure certain outcomes e.g. environmental on frequent basis, time-lag between activities and outcomes etc.), in practice these can be complemented by some indicators pertaining to levels of compliance (specifically decreasing non-compliance, particularly among high-risk groups).

- *Evidence: performance indicators as officially adopted and publicised*

3.   In order to determine the relative importance of different risks, the adequacy of different methods, the potential and real effectiveness of actions, it is essential to take as basis, as much as possible, reliable science. When science is not conclusive enough and uncertainty is significant, decisions on risk assessment, choice of approach, resource allocation etc. should be transparent about this uncertainty, and the choices that have been made. Likewise, if a decision is reached to treat a given issue with more (or less) intensity than its risk level estimated based on scientific evidence would warrant, there should be full transparency and clarity on what values this decision was based on, and what trade-offs were accepted as part of this decision. Science cannot be the only guide to policy decisions, and often enough uncertainty makes it indispensable to make judgment calls anyway – but clarity about values, criteria and trade-offs is essential to ensure that the decisions are evidence-based, and can be properly assessed by stakeholders. The definition of "science" should here be understood to not be limited only to natural sciences, but to include also social sciences.

Sub-criterion 1.4. Effectiveness evaluations are implemented in practice, and really inform choices in terms of inspection and enforcement structures, methods, resources and tools

In order for inspections and enforcement to be genuinely evidence-based, evaluations of effectiveness of existing practices and institutions must be regularly conducted – and actions taken on the basis of these evaluations. Such evaluations would consider the evolution of performance indicators over several years, trends in improvement or worsening of key indicators of over time (whether there are any inflexion points), comparison with other jurisdictions (looking both at the level of indicators and at the relative trends), when possible and relevant specific surveys (which can include representative surveys of businesses or other stakeholders, but also e.g. epidemiological surveys), as well as more "qualitative" instruments (consultations with various stakeholder groups), etc.

If assessments and evaluations show the system or institution to be lacking, objectives not being met and/or costs being too high, stakeholders satisfaction being low etc., changes should be proposed and, eventually, implemented, affecting the elements that have been found wanting (institutional structures, legislation, processes, approaches, tools etc.).

- *Evidence: Official policy on evaluations, examples of public evaluations and follow up reports*

Criterion 2. Selectivity

Promoting compliance and enforcing rules should be left to market forces, private sector and civil society actions wherever possible: inspections and enforcement cannot be everywhere and address everything, and there are many other ways to achieve regulations' objectives.

Key questions:

- Are alternatives to state-led regulatory enforcement genuinely considered in the Impact Assessment process?

- Do legal and institutional mechanisms exist to enable alternatives to state-led regulatory enforcement, where appropriate?

Sub-criterion 2.1. Alternatives to state-led regulatory enforcement are genuinely considered in the Impact Assessment process

As exposed in sub-criterion 1.1, it is very important that Impact Assessment procedures genuinely consider the inspection and enforcement aspects of proposed regulatory changes, and not treat it as a given. As part of this, they should not only review needs in terms of resources and possible institutional set-ups as well as methods for inspections, but also alternatives to state-led regulatory enforcement (such as market forces, private sector and civil society actions). First, the assessment should look at whether direct inspections and enforcement would be needed at all, or whether evidence suggests that compliance could be achieved by other means (high likelihood of voluntary compliance, possibility to rely on insurance mandates, civil litigation where relevant, etc.). Second, it should consider what existing structures, mechanisms etc. could be make use of to this aim. Third, if these are found to be insufficient, but direct inspection and enforcement by state authorities appears not to be the optimal option, the assessment should lay out what changes need to be made (in legislation, institutions, resources etc.) to enable the preferred solution.[1]

When considering whether state-led regulatory enforcement is truly required, it is important to consider the question of compliance incentives: where business incentives (profitability) are to a large extent aligned with the regulation's objectives and contents,[2] there should be relatively more scrutiny about the need for enforcement resources than when regulatory objectives will clearly impose additional costs to businesses and reduce their profitability (at least in the short- or medium-term). Another key consideration is the nature of the potential harm that the regulation aims at preventing. If the harm can be remedied at a reasonable cost (i.e. remediation is not impossible, and not far more expensive than prevention), enforcement may be relatively less needed than when harm would be very expensive to remedy (far more than prevention) and/or would be *impossible* to remedy (irreversible damage).

---

1.   Whenever new regulations are introduced, it is essential to avoid this resulting in some form of more-or-less automatic creation of new enforcement powers, or (even more problematic) creation of new inspection and enforcement agency or structure. In some countries, existing legislative practices mean that new powers and responsibilities are systematically added whenever a new rule is adopted. Without prejudice to the general enforcement competence of police forces and courts, such practices should be discontinued as regards the creation of new regulatory enforcement responsibilities.

Rather, as part of the regulatory design process, drafters should consider whether state-led inspections and enforcement will be the most adequate option, whether the new regulation already is covered by existing powers and structures, and (if not) whether enforcement powers can easily and effectively be added to those of an existing structure, in a way that would avoid fragmentation and result in more coherent enforcement. Only in the negative should there be the option to create a new structure specifically tasked with enforcing this new regulation.

2.   E.g. in the case of food safety, where businesses normally have an incentive to provide safe foods for consumers. Of course, a consumer may not always know which food has potential for adverse health effects, so the information is imperfect, and the incentive is not absolute (and there are many businesses that exhibit essentially irrational behavior), hence an alignment of incentives does not ipso facto mean that enforcement is not needed. It should be noted that food safety incidents may occur from short-term intake of hazards (e.g. acute toxicity, microbiological food poisoning) or long-term intake (e.g. chronic intake of heavy metals or other chemicals).

- *Evidence:* **RIA guidelines, contents of published RIAs**

Sub-criterion 2.2. Legal and institutional mechanisms exist to enable alternatives to state-led regulatory enforcement, where appropriate – and these are effectively made use of in cases where they can be effective

Alternatives to state-led regulatory enforcement are not always preferable – be they reliance on voluntary compliance (and possibly schemes designed to incentivise such compliance, including voluntary certification, "naming and shaming" etc.), mandatory insurance, "class action" (or similar mechanisms), or reliance on civil action by individual litigants (without class action), they all have strengths and weaknesses, costs and benefits, and limitations. For instance, third-party certification combined with mandatory insurance mechanisms, backstopped by mechanisms of civil litigation between insurers and insured parties, have proven to be effective in some contexts,[3] but require a complex combination of legal infrastructure and robust insurance market, well-informed parties, and has real costs (in third-party certification, insurance premiums, expertise, litigation etc.). To take another example, class-action mechanisms have been shown by many studies to have limited effectiveness in changing corporate behaviours and improving compliance – but other, high profile cases suggest that they can have some effectiveness in other settings. In any case, they clearly have costs, and will often result in less-than-optimal distribution of costs and benefits – but they may be the best available option in some contexts (difficulty to assess where the risks may be, diffuse and uncertain risks, high costs for direct inspections and enforcement with uncertain benefits etc.).

What matters in all cases is to create the right structures (legal and institutional) so that these mechanisms can be made of in the cases where they offer the best combination of effectiveness and efficiency.

Alternatives to state-led inspections and enforcement are often seen as belonging mostly to two categories (that can be combined): mandatory third-party certification and/or insurance, and litigation-based approaches ("class action" in particular). Other possibilities exist, however, that can be described as "innovative" not necessarily because they would be really path breaking, but because they are still not widely known, or at least not widely used, or not seen as real alternatives to direct enforcement. Among these can be listed the following: "co-regulation" schemes involving state authorities "backstopping" regulation directly implemented by private-sector structures (with the state acting as a guarantee, with the ability to step in if needed, but not directly active), schemes empowering consumers (e.g. by increasing transparency of information on private sector operators in a given sector, with active efforts to make the information clearer and easier to access and understand[4]), etc. In order for such schemes to be effective, adequate resources are needed (e.g. for information), and also legal foundations (liability for private sector actors that would fail to abide by the rules, for instance). Systems that make as much use as possible of such tools, in cases where the costs of direct enforcement would seem to clearly outweigh its benefits, are likely to be more efficient and effective than others.

- *Evidence:* **Enabling legislation e.g. for collective action, insurance mandates, liability of economic operators etc. Examples of practical use of such schemes**

3.   E.g. construction regulation in France.

4 .   E.g. food hygiene ratings such as used in Denmark, the United Kingdom etc.

Criterion 3. Risk focus and proportionality

Enforcement needs to be risk-based and proportionate: the frequency of inspections and the resources employed should be proportional to the level of risk and enforcement actions should be aiming at reducing the actual risk posed by infractions.

Key questions:

- Does applicable legislation allow for risk-focus and risk-proportionality – and does it require it to be the foundation of inspection and enforcement activities?

- Does a common approach to risk assessment and risk management exist, or at least similar understanding and practices across most regulatory domains?

- Is the majority of inspections proactive, the targeting of inspections effectively based on risk, including the management of complaints and reactive inspections?

- Are enforcement decisions effectively based on risk-proportionality?

- Are risks, risk management strategy and risk-based enforcement approach are clearly and actively communicated to all stakeholders, with a view to manage expectations and improve outcomes?

Sub-criterion 3.1. Applicable legislation allows for risk-focus and risk-proportionality – and requires it to be the foundation of inspection and enforcement activities

In order for inspections and enforcement to be effectively founded on risk-focus and risk-proportionality, it is first needed that these actually be allowed by legislation (and broader case law). In a number of countries, legal wording and/or legal interpretation make it very difficult to properly use risk-based approaches, because they are understood to mandate full enforcement of every norm, without any discretion in targeting and response. In practice, there is overwhelming evidence that there cannot be effective, universal coverage by inspections, and that enforcement decisions are never without any discretion (since there is always some discretion in determining whether there is a violation, and what it is). Such legal doctrines or rules, however, make it very difficult for inspection and enforcement institutions to develop risk-based approaches where discretion is openly embraced, and organised – even though in practice they allow to move from arbitrary selectivity (through lack of time and resources) to meaningful selectivity (based on risk).

The first need is thus to have legislation that explicitly and clearly allows for selectivity in inspection visits (not requiring universal control) and for differentiation in enforcement response (allowing for adaptation to circumstances and proportionality, as long as criteria are clear). Further, it is even better if legislation not only allows but actually requires the use of risk-based approaches. Evidence suggests that many inspection and enforcement institutions are reluctant to reduce their discretionary power, and thus resist the introduction of risk-based approaches, which replace unbounded individual discretion by clear criteria for targeting and response. Having policies, laws and regulations that mandate them is thus clearly good practice.

- *Evidence: framework or sector-specific legislation contents regarding discretion, risk proportionality*

Sub-criterion 3.2. A common approach to risk assessment and risk management exists, or at least similar understanding and practices across most regulatory domains

Allowing and even mandating the use of risk-based approaches is insufficient if there is no proper understanding of what such approaches actually mean, and how to implement them. Risk should be properly understood as combining the likelihood of some adverse event, with the potential magnitude and severity of the consequences of this event (i.e. "high risk" is very different from "high likelihood of violation"). It is thus important to have an official definition of risk that applies across all regulatory areas. In order to make co-ordination of actions between different inspection structures more effective, to allow for better allocation of resources across different fields and regulatory areas, and to allow for more meaningful risk-proportionality, it is very useful to have a common approach to risk assessment and risk management across government. This should include a unified definition of risk, as well as common tools and methods to assess and rate risks, and to determine the appropriate response. Of course, sufficient customisation for the needs of specific areas must be allowed. If they are not wholly shared across different institutions or functions, there should at least be a sufficiently high level of similarity to allow for coherence across the regulatory system.

- *Evidence: official document(s) on risk assessment and risk management*

Sub-criterion 3.3. Majority of inspections are proactive, targeting of inspections is effectively based on risk, including the management of complaints and reactive inspections

Risk-focus should not only be mandated by official guidance (and if possible by legislation), it also should take place in practice. This means that the vast majority of inspections should be proactive, with their targeting based on risk assessment (itself relying on data on different sectors and establishments). Risk factors taken into account for this targeting should include at least intrinsic risk of the activity, scope of operations, vulnerability factors (location, population served) if relevant, and past track record. Even when receiving complaints or other information, a risk-based methodology should be used to determine whether to conduct reactive inspections: reliability or credibility of the information, seriousness of the risk outlined in the complaint, past track record (previous complaints), etc. Reactive inspections should remain a minority of the total, and systematic response by an inspection (one complaint, one inspection) should be excluded. At the same time, a base-level frequency of inspections can be required to maintain supervision credibility. Also, incidentally, an inspection may be needed to provide the regulator with sufficient insight into current market developments or a firm's market initiatives, even if the ex-ante risk assessment does not mandate the inspection.

- *Evidence: official guidelines on targeting, annual reports with data on inspection activities and targeting (with data on different risk groups)*

Sub-criterion 3.4. Enforcement decisions are effectively based on risk-proportionality

Risk-proportionality in taking enforcement decisions is at least as important as targeting inspections based on risk assessment. When assessing the situation in an establishment, inspectors should consider not only whether there are any violations, but whether these violations are part of a pattern, whether they reflect deliberate reckless behaviour or result from mistakes that the operator is ready to correct at the earliest, and crucially whether these violations actually create serious risks for the public welfare (safety, health, environment etc.) – and, if so, the magnitude of these risks. As much as possible, there should be official guidance clarifying how risk proportionality works and how enforcement decisions should be taken, so as to increase transparency and reduce uncertainty.

- *Evidence: official guidelines on risk-proportional enforcement, annual reports with data on enforcement decisions and analysis/trends*

*Sub-criterion 3.6. **Risks, risk management strategy and risk-based enforcement approach are clearly and actively communicated to all stakeholders, with a view to manage expectations and improve outcomes***

Risk-communication is essential to any risk management strategy. In the case of inspections and enforcement activities this means in particular transparency about risk criteria to make discretion legitimate, clarity about limitations in risk prevention to ensure expectations are correctly managed, and better information about key risks so as to improve compliance with key requirements and improve outcomes. Such information should target all key stakeholders: business operators, consumers, workers, citizens. A key element of risk communication is to make it clear that managing risk cannot be done by inspectors alone. Strong information and outreach is a key element of success.

- *Evidence: **official policy and evidence of outreach efforts***

Criterion 4. Responsive regulation

Enforcement should be based on "responsive regulation" principles: inspection enforcement actions should be modulated depending on the profile and behaviour of specific businesses.

Key questions:

- Does applicable legislation allow for differentiated (responsive) enforcement and provides an appropriate framework for discretion (allowing for it, but within bounds, and with accountability)?

- Is the gradation of available sanctions adequate to allow credible deterrence through escalation of sanctions ("light" enough to be used when needed, "strong" enough to outweigh potential profits from non-compliance)?

- Is there a clear distinction, but also effective articulation, between regulatory activities focusing on promoting compliance (including, when needed, by using enforcement powers), and law-enforcement activities focusing on fighting crime (conducted by police forces, public prosecutors etc.)?

- Do enforcement practices differentiate responses based on regulated subjects track record (and treat newly established businesses distinctly), risk assessment, effectiveness of different options?

Sub-criterion 4.1. Applicable legislation allows for (or, at least, does not prohibit) differentiated (responsive) enforcement and provides an appropriate framework for discretion (allowing for it, but within bounds, and with accountability)

There is strong evidence that responsive regulation delivers better outcomes than uniform sanctioning of each and every violation – but laws and legal practices do not always allow for it. It is thus indispensable that legislation explicitly allows for differentiation in enforcement response (from simple warning to full weight of sanctions or prosecution) depending on the circumstances (seriousness of the violations in terms of risk, track record, overall situation in establishment, readiness to comply and improve, intent or lack thereof, dissimulation or openness etc.). Enforcement discretion should be clearly allowed (as it will anyway exist in practice), but also restrained by the application of principles and criteria (in particular risk-proportionality). There should also be requirements for enforcement structures to be accountable for their decisions (public guidelines for inspectors on decision making, annual reporting on enforcement actions, including justification).

- *Evidence: contents of applicable framework and/or sector-specific legislation regulating enforcement in enforcement decisions, secondary legislation and/or guidelines on how to exercise it*

Sub-criterion 4.2. The gradation of available sanctions is adequate to allow credible deterrence through escalation of sanctions ("light" enough to be used when needed, "strong" enough to outweigh potential profits from non-compliance)

In order for the enforcement response to be credible, and to achieve some deterrence effect, the potential sanctions must be sufficiently strong to outweigh the potential benefits from violations – but they should be sufficiently flexible that there is a credible threat that inspectors and enforcement agencies will actually use them. If only very severe sanctions (e.g. shutting down the establishment) are available, then they will very rarely be used (at least in most jurisdictions) because the economic and social consequences, and potential political backlash, would be considerable. Legislation should thus foresee a range of differentiated responses, including e.g. simple warning, official notice of improvement with inclusion in a public list or display of inspection results (using the incentive of negative advertisement to drive behaviour change), through administrative fines, up to prosecution, closure, potentially punitive damages or compensation of undue profits if and as applicable etc. At the same time, inspectorates should ensure that follow up inspections are carried out to ensure full compliance in cases of the use of "softer" responses (i.e. follow up inspections after issuing a warning).

- *Evidence: provisions in framework and/or sector-specific legislation empowering officials to apply sanctions, secondary legislation and/or guidance clarifying the range of possible decisions*

Sub-criterion 4.3. Clear distinction, but also effective articulation, between regulatory activities focusing on promoting compliance, and law-enforcement activities focusing on fighting crime

In order to develop an effective and efficient, risk-based, responsive inspection and enforcement system, it is essential that its activities and goals be distinguished from that of the crime-fighting, law enforcement system.[1] The former focuses on promoting compliance among the vast majority, which are either voluntarily compliant or likely to become so given adequate incentives (information, legitimacy of rules and institutions, social norms, and deterrence). The latter targets those that are clearly criminal and do not react to other incentives – and it should have the right instruments at its disposal, which are fully distinct from those of regulatory inspections and enforcement. Articulating clearly this distinction in legislation, institutions and practices is important to develop inspection and enforcement institutions that gain legitimacy among and active co-operation from those they regulate. Having effective information exchange, and clarity on how to share responsibilities between these two types of enforcement, is just as essential in order to address the whole spectrum of business operators, risks and violations. Regulatory inspections should be clearly distinct from law enforcement in the criminal sense, but they need a link to this law enforcement in order for the system to avoid gaps.[2]

Fulfilling this criterion can be achieved in a number of ways, but fundamentally it requires that the mission of inspections and enforcement agencies be seen as the *maximisation of compliance levels*, and not the systematic detection and punishment of each and every violation. It thus requires that legislation gives these agencies appropriate discretion to handle different situations in different ways, including to decline to punish certain violations if they consider that they pose very little risk and can be handled without formal enforcement.

- *Evidence: official government vision, mandates of inspections and enforcement institutions (official statutes, strategy documents, annual reports etc.)*

1.   This should *not* be understood to mean that it is in inadequate for an inspections and enforcement agency to have enforcement powers (including prosecutorial powers in countries where this is possible and where criminal prosecutions are an important enforcement tool). What matters is primarily a distinction of missions and purposes. Criminal prosecution *as part of regulatory enforcement* will be one of a series of tools in a "responsive regulation" framework, where it represents the maximal escalation for particularly egregious cases. The objective overall remains, however, compliance. By contrast, the specific purpose of law-enforcement as conducted by police forces focusing on criminal cases, and public prosecutors, is specifically to detect and punish crime – and not primarily to increase average compliance levels.

2.   As per above, the link can be internal (in house prosecutorial powers) as well as external (information exchange with law enforcement bodies, and possibility to "escalate" matters by transferring cases to the public prosecutor).

Sub-criterion 4.4. Enforcement practices differentiate responses based on regulated subject track record (and treat newly established businesses distinctly), risk assessment, effectiveness of different options

In practice, responsive enforcement requires differentiation based on the track record of the operator, on the risk assessment (damages that the violation has already caused and/or is likely to cause, considering also the broader compliance context in the establishment), and on the potential effectiveness of different options. The latter means considering the impact of the enforcement response on future compliance both inside the establishment (likely staff and management response) and outside of it (exemplarity effect). Since individual inspectors cannot be expected to have full knowledge of all the experience and evidence that could be relevant to choose between different possible responses, the availability of sufficiently detailed guidance is indispensable – combined with strong professional skills to properly assess the situation on site. Having detailed guidance is in any case insufficient – ensuring that the actual practice of inspectors and the decisions of their management correspond to a responsive approach is essential.

- *Evidence: official policy documents, annual reports data and analysis*

Criterion 5. Long-term vision

Governments should adopt policies on regulatory enforcement and inspections: clear objectives should be set and institutional mechanisms set up with clear objectives and a long-term road-map.

Key questions:

- Has an official vision, strategy and/or legal framework been adopted for regulatory enforcement and inspections, setting goals and objectives, key principles?

- Are there mechanisms and practices (including, but not limited to, Impact Assessment) to avoid or limit the occurrence of "Risk-Regulation Reflex" situations and decisions?

- Does the long-term vision have practical effects, and does it guide key reforms, legislation and decisions? Is an institutional framework in place to ensure this, avoid short-term policy swings?

Sub-criterion 5.1. An official vision, strategy and/or legal framework has been adopted for regulatory enforcement and inspections, setting goals, objectives and key principles

For the inspections and enforcement system to properly develop, it needs a long-term framework with clear goals and principles, to shield it from short-term, conflicting priorities. This can be adopted in different ways – government programme, legislation, etc., but it should be sufficiently strong and stable to play its role. This document should include principles, goals and objectives for the overall system.

- *Evidence: official vision, strategy document or other framework*

Sub-criterion 5.2. Mechanisms and practices (including, but not limited to, Impact Assessment) to avoid or limit the occurrence of "Risk-Regulation Reflex" situations and decisions

The "Risk Regulation Reflex" is the short description of a phenomenon that is too frequent: rash reactions following some accident or the emergence of a new risk, whereby state authorities urgently adopt new regulations, inspections and enforcement measures, without proper consideration of the extent of the risk, the adequacy of the proposed solutions and their costs. The "reflex" is driven by political considerations, the need "to be seen doing something", and produces major costs, unintended negative consequences etc. A good, risk-based inspections and enforcement system needs to be protected from such "reflex" decisions. This includes, of course, Impact Assessment mechanisms (which apply to the production of new regulations), but should be complemented by measures (in law, government programmes, practices etc.) that also exclude "Risk Regulation Reflex" responses in the inspection and enforcement sphere (which could mean suddenly deciding e.g. universal inspections in a given sector following some accident, without consideration of data, risks etc.).

- *Evidence: official policy or government vision on managing risk, responding to incidents and crises*

Sub-criterion 5.3. The long-term vision has practical effects, informs key reforms, legislation and decisions. An institutional framework is in place to ensure this and avoid short-term policy swings

Having an official vision or strategy is not sufficient if it is not translated into practice. It is crucial that the principles and goals stated in the framework document are respected when new legislation is adopted, institutional changes decided upon, or strategic decisions made within inspecting structures. To this aim, it is helpful to have a dedicated institution in charge of promoting the implementation of the strategy, helping inspecting structures in understanding and applying it, and ensuring that it is taken into account in new legislation, reforms etc.

- *Evidence: institutional mechanism in place to ensure implementation of long-term vision or strategy*

Criterion 6. Co-ordination and consolidation

Inspection functions should be co-ordinated and, where needed, consolidated: less duplication and overlaps will ensure better use of public resources, minimise burden on regulated subjects, and maximise effectiveness.

Key questions:

- Is the issue of institutional mandates, co-ordination and consolidation taken into account at the regulatory drafting stage and in the Impact Assessment process?

- Is duplication of functions avoided and are mandates and responsibilities clear (between different institutions, between national and local levels)?

- Do different inspection and enforcement structures share information and records, participate in joint alert systems, co-ordinate "on the ground" – particularly in related regulatory areas?

- Are mechanisms in place or being introduced to increase efficiency through better information sharing, agencies acting as "eyes and ears" for others? Are re-inspections of the same issue avoided, as well as duplicated reporting?

- Are allocation of resources and strategic planning done taking into account all structures working in a given regulatory area?

---

*Sub-criterion 6.1. **The issue of institutional mandates, co-ordination and consolidation is taken into account at the regulatory drafting stage and in the Impact Assessment process***

Avoiding the proliferation of different inspecting institutions, ensuring clarity and coherence, preventing the emergence of areas of conflicting competence are all essential. To this aim, during the drafting of new regulations (including the Impact Assessment process) there should be particular attention given to which institutions or structures already have inspection and enforcement competences in the fields under consideration, who would be in charge of implementing the new regulations, and ensuring that the result is coherent, clear and avoids overlaps or fragmentation.

- *Evidence: **RIA guidelines and contents of published RIAs***

*Sub-criterion 6.2. **Duplication of functions is avoided and mandates and responsibilities are clear (between different institutions, between national and local levels)***

In order for the inspection system to be clear for regulated actors, efficient (no duplicate cost or burden), and effective (no dispersion of information and efforts, no co-ordination problems), there needs to be as much as possible unicity of functions – one institution responsible for an entire regulatory area (e.g. food safety, product safety etc.), or at least for a regulatory area in a given sector (e.g. primary food production). When several institutions are involved or cover related fields (e.g. public health and hygiene, occupational health, environment), there should be clarity as to who is responsible for particular regulations, establishments etc. Such clarity should also be ensured between different geographic levels (national or federal, regional, local etc.) so that establishments are not subject to repeated (potentially conflicting) inspections, and public resources wasted on uncoordinated and duplicating activities. Because it is rare that an inspections and enforcement system is fully clear and streamlined, given that institutions have typically developed over many years and as a result of separate policy initiatives, it is important for governments (or regional authorities, where they have responsibility for inspections) to undertake initiatives to review existing functions and institutions, and seek to streamline and consolidate them, or at least clarify the roles and responsibilities, where appropriate.

- *Evidence: **overview document on inspection functions, official initiatives to consolidate or clarify them***

*Sub-criterion 6.3. **Different inspection and enforcement structures share information and records, participate in joint alert systems, co-ordinate "on the ground" – particularly in related regulatory areas***

Even assuming an optimal split of responsibilities ensuring maximum clarity, there will remain different structures in charge of regulatory fields that are distinct but related – and in any case evidence shows that (non-)compliance in one area is often a predictor of (non-)compliance in another, thus sharing of intelligence is essential to improve risk-based targeting, efficiency and effectiveness. To this aim, good inspections and enforcement practices include joint alert systems,[1] systematic (or, as a second best, upon request) sharing of information and records on establishments under supervision, and co-ordination of inspections (sharing of plans, joint inspections, etc.).

- *Evidence: existing systems (joint alert, information sharing etc.), institutional mechanisms, joint plans of inspections*

*Sub-criterion 6.4. **Mechanisms are in place or being introduced to increase efficiency through better information sharing, agencies acting as "eyes and ears" for others – re-inspections of the same issue are avoided, as well as duplicated reporting***

Going further than sharing of formal data and records, different inspection structures can collaborate to increase their efficiency and their ability to assess risks by agreeing to act as "eyes and ears" for each other. In some cases, it can be by agreeing on a "lead agency" that will be the one doing regular inspections in a given sector, and call in others if it spots problems in their specific field of competence. In other cases, it can be by giving to all inspectors in several (or all) structures a basic knowledge of other inspection fields so that they can spot potential major risks during their visits, and alert other structures about them.

In addition, further improvements in efficiency and reductions in burden can be achieved by putting in place norms and mechanisms prohibiting the re-inspection of one and the same issue by two different structures, and requiring all state structures to share information (and thus prohibiting duplicate reporting requirements, what has been called in some countries the "tell it once only" rule).

- *Evidence: official policies or memoranda of understanding between agencies, documented processes and procedures, contents of staff training curriculum*

---

1.   Such as RASFF and RAPEX for the EU in food and product safety.

Sub-criterion 6.5. Allocation of resources and strategic planning are done taking into account all structures working in a given regulatory area

As outlined in Criterion 1, allocation of resources between inspection and enforcement areas should be done based on evidence, and (as per criterion 3) in a way proportional to risk. When doing so, it is essential to consider all the different institutions, structures, levels, etc. that may be involved, not just one given agency. In most cases, a number of different structures will be involved to some extent in implementing regulations in a given area, and when assessing available and required resources it is indispensable to have this broader picture, and not end up doing multiple allocation of resources for what is in essence the same (or closely related) issue(s). This entails, when long-term or mid-term strategic reviews or planning are undertaken (at whichever level this takes place) at the very least taking into account the staffing, expertise, technical resource and (if possible) budget allocations of all the institutions that are involved in supervising a given regulatory domain. The same holds true when benchmarking exercises are conducted comparing the situation in one jurisdiction with another: meaningful comparisons cannot be done without taking into account an entire regulatory domain, and not just one single institution, if more than one institution is involved.[2]

- *Evidence: guidelines on strategic planning/review, contents of strategic planning/review documents*

2.   E.g. in occupational health and safety or food safety there are frequently more than one institution involved in inspections and enforcement. A proper review or planning exercise will need to at least take into consideration all their resources (even if planning is not joint, at least it should incorporate the existence of the other institutions involved).

Criterion 7. Transparent governance

Governance structures and human resources policies for regulatory enforcement should support transparency, professionalism, and results-oriented management. Execution of regulatory enforcement should be independent from political influence, and compliance promotion efforts should be rewarded.

Key questions:

- Is senior management of enforcement and inspection institutions appointed in a transparent way, based on professional competence, minimising political interference?

- Do key decisions, changes in processes, procedures and structures require collegial decisions and/or external scrutiny, avoiding excessive instability and discretionary managerial power?

- Are stakeholders consulted and represented in the governance of inspection and enforcement institutions, particularly strategic ones?

- Do inspection and enforcement structures have missions, powers, procedures and funding mechanisms that exclude conflicts of interest and conflicting goals?

- Are decisions at all levels based on transparent criteria and processes, allowing for consistency in enforcement decisions, and accountability?

- Do strategic decisions and changes require political approval (legislative, executive), while operational decisions are made "at arm's length" and shielded from political interference?

Sub-criterion 7.1. Senior management of enforcement and inspection institutions is appointed in a transparent way, based on professional competence, minimising political interference

Chief executives and other senior managers in charge of inspection and enforcement structures should be selected for their professional competence, specifically as managers (and not only or mainly as technical specialists in the field of inspection). Selections based on political connections, patronage or other connections need to be excluded as much as possible. To this aim, selection and appointment processes should be transparent, including clear criteria, open advertisement, balanced selection committee rather than appointment by one sole senior political official without scrutiny, as is often the case. All possible care should be taken to minimise political interference.

- *Evidence: policies and procedures for recruitment of senior management*

Sub-criterion 7.2. Key decisions, changes in processes, procedures and structures require collegial decisions and/or external scrutiny, avoiding excessive instability and discretionary managerial power

Even with the best possible process for selecting managers, ensuring continuity of institutional practices, professionalism, strategic focus requires that senior managers have only limited powers to impose changes single-handed to inspection institutions. Significant changes to e.g. internal structure, strategic goals, indicators, risk-management and compliance strategies etc. should all require decisions by a collegial body – preferably an external, independent board.

- *Evidence: official statutes and other official documents prescribing governance of inspections and enforcement institutions*

Sub-criterion 7.3. Stakeholders are consulted and represented in the governance of inspection and enforcement institutions, particularly strategic ones

Representation of stakeholders (businesses, civil society organisations etc.) in the management board (or similar structure) has considerable added value as it ensures greater transparency, increased legitimacy, and ensures that the institution remains attuned to public concerns. Consultation of stakeholders should be the norm at least for strategic decisions (definition of goals and indicators, adoption of risk-management or compliance strategy etc.) – just as consulting stakeholders is required in all forms of Impact Assessment processes. Key strategic decisions in inspections and enforcement have at least as much relevance to stakeholders as regulations themselves, and can benefit as much from their input. This can be done through formal *ad hoc* consultations and/or through permanent representatives in a board-type structure.

- *Evidence: official statutes and other official documents prescribing governance of inspections and enforcement institutions, annual reports*

Sub-criterion 7.4. Inspection and enforcement structures have missions, powers, procedures and funding mechanisms that exclude, to the extent possible, conflicts of interest and conflicting goals

There are many ways in which mandates and missions, or funding mechanisms, can create conflicts of interest for inspection and enforcement. For instance, if funding is linked to the number of inspections, the agency will have an incentive to increase volume of visits, regardless of risk, efficiency and effectiveness considerations. If an agency both issues licences and does subsequent compliance checks, but issuing licences is revenue-raising, it will have an incentive to disregard compliance issues when issuing, at the risk of safety or other public interests. If an agency both provides payable, competitive services (for which it competes with other providers) and has regulatory enforcement powers, it will have an undue advantage over competitors, as it can put pressure on regulated entities to purchase its services. Finally, when the same entity has several unrelated goals that compete for the same resources, it is essential to have some high-level guidance on how to allocate resources between them. If one of the goals requires co-operation from regulated subjects, while the other may create conflicts with them (because of a different alignment of incentives), it would be needed to assess how best to manage this internal contradiction (splitting functions or teams, prioritising one of the goals, changing methods). If conflicting objectives are assigned to separate institutions which are supposed to co-ordinate with each other, it is also needed to assess how such conflicts should be managed.

- *Evidence: legislation, official documents (statutes etc.), budget documents, annual reports*

Sub-criterion 7.5. Decisions at all levels are made based on transparent criteria and processes, allowing for consistency in enforcement decisions, and accountability

Opaque and confidential decisions should be avoided. It is essential that all decisions be founded on clear criteria (e.g. risk proportionality), transparent processes, with possibilities to appeal etc. The aim is not only to ensure consistency between different officials, regions etc. – but also accountability, by allowing assessing the outcomes of decisions, knowing who took them, on which basis, etc.

- *Evidence: official guidelines and annual reports*

*Sub-criterion 7.6. **Strategic decisions and changes require political approval (legislative, executive) – but operational decisions are made "at arm's length" and shielded from political interference***

Strategic decisions include defining the institution's goals and objectives, performance indicators, risk and compliance strategies, methodological documents (risk assessment and targeting, enforcement management, check-lists, etc.), structure, high-level resource allocation, terms of reference of staff etc. It is normal to have these require approval by executive or legislative branches of government, as appropriate. Operational decisions, however, which *implement* these strategic decisions (planning and targeting of inspections, allocation of tasks and staff, enforcement decisions) should be left strictly to the professional staff and management, without any interference from political office-holders (or other parties). It is essential to have both legal rules, institutional mechanisms and practices to this effect.

- *Evidence: official legislation and statutes of inspections and enforcement institutions, annual reports*

Criterion 8. Information integration

Information and communication technologies should be used to maximise risk-focus, co-ordination and information-sharing – as well as optimal use of resources.

Key questions:

- Do inspection and enforcement structures have adequate and up-to-date data and IT tools allowing for effective risk-based planning and follow-up on previous inspections?

- Is data shared regularly between different structures and/or are records of other structures easy to look up – or, better still, is data fully integrated (single database) among different structures?

- Do information systems make use of advanced techniques e.g. automated planning, integrated resource management, mobile tools for inspectors, GIS etc.?

- Does sharing/exchange of data go beyond the "narrowly defined" inspection and enforcement field and include business registration, licensing, public health etc.?

Sub-criterion 8.1. Inspection and enforcement structures have adequate and up-to-date data and IT tools allowing for effective risk-based planning and follow-up on previous inspections

Proper risk-based targeting and effective enforcement both require adequate data and data-management tools. For the former, a comprehensive database of objects under supervision, including their fundamental characteristics in regard to risk (activities, scope, location, track record) is indispensable. For the latter, a system of case management, records and workflow management is a considerable asset. Combining both is the best option to ensure optimal efficiency and targeting.

- *Evidence: Existence of ICT systems, availability of functions and data*

Sub-criterion 8.2. Data is shared regularly between different structures and/or records of other structures are easy to look up – or, better still, data is fully integrated (single database) among different structures

As indicated in sub-criteria 6.3 and 6.4, rapid, regular information sharing is essential. ICT systems should be set up so that this happens as much as possible automatically, or at the least very easily. Ideally, several (or all) agencies should use the same database, with different agencies being responsible to fill in different data points, but all able to consult the others' data so as to improve targeting and responsiveness, and have more up-to-date data by pooling their efforts and resources.

- *Evidence: existence of systems for data exchange or data integration*

Sub-criterion 8.3. Information systems make use of advanced techniques e.g. automated planning, integrated resource management, mobile tools for inspectors, GIS etc.

To make work more efficient and targeting better, ICT tools should make use as much as possible of automated planning (based on risk criteria and risk profile of establishments recorded in the database), mobile tools for inspectors (laptop/tablet or smartphone based tools including check-lists, mobile applications or other instruments to directly record the inspection findings, look up additional information etc.), geographical information systems (GIS) to better analyse data, identify patterns, and locate the premises to be visited. The active use of search for relevant information on social networks becomes increasingly relevant.

- *Evidence: availability of automated planning functions, mobile tools, GIS systems etc.*

Sub-criterion 8.4. Sharing/exchange of data goes beyond the "narrowly defined" inspection and enforcement field and includes business registration, licensing, public health etc.

Obtaining data on contamination cases, injuries and accidents, etc. from public health and rescue services is essential to improve risk-based targeting. Likewise, to have an up-to-date list of objects under supervision requires a constant interface with business registration, licensing and permit (e.g. construction permit) systems. The more these systems can be integrated and the needed information made available, the more effective and really risk-based the inspection system can become.

- *Evidence: exchange of data with "non-inspection" services – availability of data, existence of procedures etc.*

Criterion 9. Clear and fair process

Governments should ensure clarity of rules and process for enforcement and inspections: coherent legislation to organise inspections and enforcement needs to be adopted and published, and clearly articulate rights and obligations of officials and of businesses.

Key questions:

- Is legislation on inspection and enforcement is as much as possible consolidated, and does it lay out rights, obligations, powers and procedures clearly?

- Is a comprehensive list of inspection agencies, structures or functions (as appropriate) available, and is it clear who can control which sectors and issues?

- Are there well-publicised, adequate and trusted possibilities to appeal decisions and to file complaints? Is data on appeals and complaints regularly assessed and taken into account?

- Are the decision-making processes, rights and obligations, powers of inspectors clear for all, transparent, balanced? Do they give a sound foundation for risk-proportional decisions, with adequate but bounded discretion?

Sub-criterion 9.1. Legislation on inspection and enforcement is as much as possible consolidated, and laying out rights, obligations, powers and procedures clearly

While consolidating all legislation relevant to inspection and enforcement is impossible, it is helpful to have at least key provisions about institutions, powers of officials, principles, key procedures consolidated. This allows to make it clearer and more transparent, and also to formalise best practice principles (risk management, compliance focus, responsiveness etc.) in a single document.

- *Evidence: existence of a piece of legislation covering key elements of inspections and enforcement*

Sub-criterion 9.2. A comprehensive list of inspection agencies, structures or functions (as appropriate) is available, and it is clear who can control which sectors and issues

Knowing which institutions are empowered to inspect and control, on which topics, is essential for predictability, for regulated subjects to exercise their rights, and for the public to demand accountability. Too often, this is nearly impossible because of the proliferation of structures and powers. Consolidating this into a single official document is a considerable help.

- *Evidence: availability of a consolidated list of inspection services*

Sub-criterion 9.3. There are well publicised, adequate and trusted possibilities to appeal decisions and to file complaints – and data on appeals and complaints is regularly assessed and taken into account

Appealing against decisions by inspectors tends to be done only reluctantly because regulated subjects fear spoiling their relationship with institutions that are bound to continue inspecting them in the future. This is all the more reason to make appeal procedures easy, and give regulated subjects possibilities (e.g. through administrative review boards or similar) to have their case reviewed rapidly and independently from the administration that took the original decision. Likewise, possibilities for trusted, anonymous complaints against abuse need to be present. Conversely, citizens, consumers, workers etc. should have well-publicised, simple to use possibilities to file complaints against regulated subjects, and know how they are being handled (while, as indicated in criterion 3, these should be reviewed in a risk proportional way).

- *Evidence: appeal and complaints processes description, data on use of appeals and complaints, evidence of follow up through annual reports and/or strategy documents*

Sub-criterion 9.4. Decision-making processes, rights and obligations, powers of inspectors are clear for all, transparent, balanced – giving a sound foundation for risk-proportional decisions, with adequate but bounded discretion

Both in framework legislation for inspections (if it exists) and specific legislation for individual inspection structures, the processes for decision-making, powers and rights of inspectors (and their limits), rights and obligations of regulated subjects, as well as appeal and complaint procedures, should all be made clear. They should be easily accessible. It is also important that, while inspectors should have sufficient powers to effectively fulfil their duties, there are also adequate limitations to avoid abuse and protect fundamental rights of regulated subjects. Explicit reference should be made to proportionality and risk, and clarifications given on the limits of the exercise of discretion.

- *Evidence: processes, powers and rights as defined in primary and secondary legislation and other official documents*

Criterion 10. Compliance promotion

Transparency and compliance should be promoted through the use of appropriate instruments such as guidance, toolkits and checklists.

Key questions:

- Is promoting and supporting compliance seen as a duty of inspection and enforcement structures – avoiding reliance on an "everyone should know the law" approach, or seeing advice and guidance as activities that should be left to private consultants?

- Do regulators, inspection and enforcement structures actively and regularly analyse barriers to compliance, and work to overcome them, in particular as they relate to information?

- Are information, advice and guidance delivered through a variety of complementary tools – clear, practical and easy-to-find guidance documents – active outreach – on-the-ground advice?

- Do legal foundations exist for the practice of "assured advice" and is it being used as much as possible to increase regulatory certainty?

- Is performance of inspection and enforcement structures, and of the overall regulatory system, assessed in terms of compliance levels (and public welfare outcomes), not in terms of number of violations detected (and punished)?

Sub-criterion 10.1. Promoting and supporting compliance is seen as a duty of inspection and enforcement structures rather than relying on an "everyone should know the law" approach, or seeing advice and guidance as activities that should be left to private consultants

All too often continues to prevail the view that the duty to know the law is on regulated subjects alone, whereas this legal principle was stated in times when the number, length and complexity of laws was but a fraction of what they are today. Likewise, the absence of efforts to actively inform regulated subjects and promote compliance by clear, practical advice is often excused by claiming that such activities should be left to the private sector, to consulting firms. Neither of these arguments is valid.

In a time when the state is, in response to new risks and growing demands, imposing numerous and complex regulations, it is inadequate to just assume that business operators or citizens can inform themselves and understand what is expected without any assistance. Rather, promoting and supporting compliance should be a key priority and function of inspection and enforcement structures, this should be anchored in legislation and in the official mandates of these different structures, and significant resources should be allocated to develop and spread guidance and information to regulated subjects, particularly those lacking the resources to obtain or understand the information themselves, e.g. SMEs.

- *Evidence: government vision on inspections, framework legislation, strategy documents, etc.*

Sub-criterion 10.2. Regulators, inspection and enforcement structures actively and regularly analyse barriers to compliance, and work to overcome them, in particular as they relate to information

Improving compliance requires the analysis of what hinders it – which can be lack of information and understanding, insufficient resources, or poor regulatory design. Inspection and enforcement structures should give feedback about regulatory design and resource issues to policymakers. They can also directly tackle information gaps. Thus, reviewing and assessing barriers to compliance (using their own inspectors' findings) is essential, and should be a core activity.

- *Evidence: annual reports and strategy documents*

Sub-criterion 10.3. Information, advice and guidance are delivered through a variety of complementary tools – clear, practical and easy-to-find guidance documents – active outreach – on-the-ground advice

Different channels need to be used for different issues and audiences, and inspection structures should use all of them actively. Practical and clear guidance documents should be prepared covering the most widespread business activities and regulatory issues, and the key risks – and be actively disseminated, including through consolidated internet portals (dispersed information being often impossible to find). Active outreach to new businesses, business associations, sectors where most difficulties are observed etc. should be organised, using visits, conferences, web-based information, etc. Inspection visits should be used as key moments to inform, explain and advise.

Guidance must be elaborated and given with great care. Guidance must not diverge from the path set out by the overlaying regulatory framework. Correlation between the guidance and the regulatory framework must be ensured. Guidance, toolkits and checklists must not constitute over-implementation (gold-plating) of the overlaying regulatory framework.

- *Evidence: existence of guidance documents, outreach portals – annual reports on outreach activities*

Sub-criterion 10.4. Legal foundations exist for the practice of "assured advice" and it is being used as much as possible to increase regulatory certainty

The practice of "assured advice" consists in giving legal guarantees to regulated subjects that, if they follow the advice officially given by their regulator, they will not be held in breach of their duties, even if at a later point another official reaches a different conclusion. At most, if it is found that the original advice was indeed wrong (or if the rules have changed), the regulated entity will have to put itself in compliance, but it will not face liability or sanctions. Such practice exists in a number of countries under different names,[1] but is often resisted, and can be made impossible (or at least difficult) by conflicting legal provisions. It is thus highly advisable to give it a sound legal foundation, and even make it a legal requirement for inspectorates to be bound by their own advice.[2] However, this practice must be designed in a way that it does not limit the willingness of the inspectors to share their opinion in more informal communications with the regulated subjects. Also, providing this kind of advice should not take off the responsibility to make their own assessment on how best to comply with regulations from inspected subjects. When provided with an "assured advice", regulated subject should not need to follow conflicting advice from other sources. Hence, the "assured advice" should be made available to other enforcement authorities, e.g. through a shared information system. While it is rarely possible to have every advice be "assured advice", the goal should be to have this be the case as much as possible, to improve regulatory certainty and improve compliance levels by giving strong incentives to regulated subjects to ask for advice and follow it. It needs to be clear when the inspector gives general advice and when he gives "assured advice".

- *Evidence: framework or other primary legislation (or, in its absence, secondary legislation) foreseeing the possibility of "assured advice" – existence of institutional mechanisms to provide it[3]*

---

1. E.g. "rescrit fiscal" in France for tax matters, https://www.service-public.fr/particuliers/vosdroits/F13551.

2. As is the case in Lithuania as per the Law on Public Administration.

3. E.g. the "Primary Authority" scheme in the United Kingdom.

Criterion 11. Professionalism

Inspectors should be trained and managed to ensure professionalism, integrity, consistency and transparency: this requires substantial training focusing not only on technical but also on generic inspection skills, and official guidelines for inspectors to help ensure consistency and fairness.

Key questions:

- Is the profession of "inspector"[1] defined as such, with a combination of technical (field-specific) skills and "core" competencies linked to risk management, compliance promotion etc.? Is professionalism the foundation for risk-based discretion?

- Is training for inspection and enforcement staff conducted both upon recruitment, and on-the-job throughout their career, to ensure both up-to-date knowledge and adequate methods?

- Are competency of staff members, and overall capacity of the organisations they work in, regularly assessed? And are efforts made to continuously enhance them?

1.   The name can change from country to country.

Sub-criterion 11.1. The profession of "inspector" is defined as such, with a combination of technical (field-specific) skills and "core" competencies linked to risk management, compliance promotion etc. Professionalism is the foundation for risk-based discretion

Inspecting and enforcing regulations is a profession, which is distinct from that of being a technical specialist (of specific environmental or health issues, for instance). While it *requires* technical knowledge and skills, they are but a part of what is needed. Defining the profession of inspector as one distinct from that of technical specialist is an important element, and with it goes the need to delineate what competences are needed for inspectors: understanding and managing risks, communicating and advising, promoting and supporting compliance, investigating etc. Only professional inspectors, with a full understanding of their mission and of the tools that can be used to fulfil it (and of their limitations) can adequately exercise discretion. Such a framework for the inspection profession should be officially stated, and form the basis for recruitment practices, job descriptions, training, professional assessments and performance evaluation for staff.

- *Evidence: official document(s) defining the role of inspectors, the core elements required in terms of professional qualification*

Sub-criterion 11.2. Training for inspection and enforcement staff is conducted both upon recruitment, and on-the-job throughout their career, to ensure both up-to-date knowledge and adequate methods

Based on the professional framework described above, training needs to be developed and conducted for inspection staff, both initially (before or after recruitment) and during their career. Initial training can be done in a university context (with specific courses) or outside of it, and there are a variety of approaches that can be taken for on the job training. What is crucial is to ensure that inspectors receive both the adequate technical training (and regular "refreshers") but also training on their function and how to best exercise it (and updates on new findings, methods etc. during their career).

- *Evidence: official document(s) on training, including curriculum – annual reports*

Sub-criterion 11.3. Competency of staff members, and overall capacity of the organisations they work in, are regularly assessed – and efforts are made to continuously enhance them

Requiring competencies and providing training is insufficient without regular assessment. This should be used to identify gaps and needs, and achieve improvements. Thus, assessments should be made not only of individual capacities (self-assessment and performance evaluation), but also of the capacity of entire inspection services.

- *Evidence: official procedures and tools for assessment, annual reports (for follow up)*

Criterion 12. Reality check

Institutions in charge of inspection and enforcement, and the regulatory enforcement and inspection system overall, should deliver the performance that is expected from them – in terms of stakeholders satisfaction, of efficiency (benefits/costs), and of total effectiveness (safety, health, environmental protection etc.).

Key questions:

- Is the performance of inspection and enforcement institutions (satisfaction, efficiency, effectiveness) tracked regularly?

- Is the level of stakeholder (businesses, civil society) satisfaction and trust stable or improving?

- Is the performance in terms of safeguarding social well-being and/or controlling risks stable or improving (correcting for possible external shocks)?

- Is the efficiency (performance in terms of social well-being balanced with costs for the state and burden for regulated entities) stable or improving?

Sub-criterion 12.1. *Performance of inspection and enforcement institutions (satisfaction, efficiency, effectiveness) is tracked regularly*

Through a variety of means (surveys, official statistics or direct observation where relevant, expert evaluations, consultations etc.), key indicators of performance should be regularly tracked: satisfaction and trust (among regulated subjects, citizens, consumers, etc.), efficiency (costs to the budget, burden to regulated subjects) and effectiveness (safety, health, environmental protection etc.). While there are significant challenges and costs involved in data collection, this performance tracking is absolutely indispensable to the good functioning of the system, and its improvement – and it should form the foundation for regular assessments, reviews, changes and reforms if required.

- *Evidence: availability of data (with adequate regularity and quality)*

Sub-criterion 12.2. *Level of stakeholder (businesses, civil society) satisfaction and trust is stable or improving*

Measured through targeted surveys and/or qualitative tools (e.g. focus groups), online consultations etc. Satisfaction and trust (regarding professionalism, advice etc.) from regulated subjects to be balanced by the perspective of those that are expecting protection from regulation (citizens, consumers, workers etc.) in terms of effectiveness. Obviously, the level of stakeholder satisfaction should not be the only indicator of success (see further sub-criteria) since a lack of information among stakeholders or their bias might play a role when expressing their satisfaction. Still, it is a very important indicator.

- *Evidence: data from business surveys, focus groups etc. showing positive trends*

Sub-criterion 12.3. *Performance in terms of safeguarding social well-being and/or controlling risks is stable or improving (correcting for possible external shocks)*

Inspections and enforcement have only an indirect and limited influence on the goals they seek to further (safety, health etc.), thus their performance should be assessed in terms of trends (improving or not), and correcting for external shocks. It is also crucial to correct for the quality of data, which in some cases may be problematic, by using different sources, studies, monitoring etc., and ad hoc studies when existing ones are really insufficient.

- *Evidence: data from official sources, complemented when possible through independent studies or monitoring (including surveys), showing positive trends*

Sub-criterion 12.4. Efficiency (performance in terms of social well-being balanced with costs for the state and burden for regulated entities) is stable or improving

Inspections and enforcement create costs for the state and burden for regulated subjects – these need to be tracked regularly (including through surveys of regulated subjects) in order to balance them against performance in terms of effectiveness.

- *Evidence: data from official sources (budget costs, annual reports), complemented when possible through surveys or other measurement exercises (e.g. Standard Cost Model studies), showing positive trends*

References

OECD (2014), *Regulatory Enforcement and Inspections*, OECD Best Practice Principles for Regulatory Policy, OECD Publishing, Paris, http://dx.doi.org/10.1787/9789264208117-en. [1]

OECD (2012), *Recommendation of the Council on Regulatory Policy and Governance*, OECD Publishing, Paris, http://dx.doi.org/10.1787/9789264209022-en. [2]

OECD (2010), *Better Regulation in Europe: Netherlands 2010*, OECD Publishing, Paris, http://dx.doi.org/10.1787/9789264084568-en. [3]

ORGANISATION FOR ECONOMIC CO-OPERATION AND DEVELOPMENT

The OECD is a unique forum where governments work together to address the economic, social and environmental challenges of globalisation. The OECD is also at the forefront of efforts to understand and to help governments respond to new developments and concerns, such as corporate governance, the information economy and the challenges of an ageing population. The Organisation provides a setting where governments can compare policy experiences, seek answers to common problems, identify good practice and work to co-ordinate domestic and international policies.

The OECD member countries are: Australia, Austria, Belgium, Canada, Chile, the Czech Republic, Denmark, Estonia, Finland, France, Germany, Greece, Hungary, Iceland, Ireland, Israel, Italy, Japan, Korea, Latvia, Lithuania, Luxembourg, Mexico, the Netherlands, New Zealand, Norway, Poland, Portugal, the Slovak Republic, Slovenia, Spain, Sweden, Switzerland, Turkey, the United Kingdom and the United States. The European Union takes part in the work of the OECD.

OECD Publishing disseminates widely the results of the Organisation's statistics gathering and research on economic, social and environmental issues, as well as the conventions, guidelines and standards agreed by its members.

OECD PUBLISHING, 2, rue André-Pascal, 75775 PARIS CEDEX 16
(42 2018 34 1 P) ISBN 978-92-64-30394-2 – 2018